50 Low-Calorie Comfort Foods

By: Kelly Johnson

Table of Contents

- Baked Zucchini Fries
- Cauliflower Mac and Cheese
- Turkey and Vegetable Chili
- Greek Yogurt Pancakes
- Spaghetti Squash Alfredo
- Sweet Potato and Black Bean Tacos
- Chicken Zoodle Soup
- Portobello Mushroom Pizza
- Baked Apple Cinnamon Oatmeal
- Grilled Lemon Herb Chicken
- Mashed Cauliflower
- Tuna-Stuffed Bell Peppers
- Skinny Lasagna Rolls
- Avocado Toast with Poached Egg
- Creamy Tomato Basil Soup
- Baked Falafel with Tahini Sauce
- Lightened-Up Shepherd's Pie
- Quinoa and Veggie Stuffed Mushrooms
- Banana Protein Pancakes
- Air-Fried Tofu Nuggets
- Chicken Lettuce Wraps
- Whole-Wheat Veggie Pizza
- Shrimp Stir-Fry with Brown Rice
- Lentil and Kale Stew
- Grilled Salmon with Mango Salsa
- Light Alfredo Pasta with Broccoli
- Sweet Potato Hash with Turkey Sausage
- Eggplant Parmesan Stacks
- Veggie-Stuffed Bell Peppers
- Black Bean and Corn Salad
- Chicken and Veggie Kebabs
- Butternut Squash Soup
- Cucumber and Hummus Wrap
- Low-Cal Chocolate Mug Cake
- Greek Salad with Grilled Chicken
- Sautéed Garlic Spinach

- Roasted Chickpeas Snack
- Cauliflower Fried Rice
- Veggie and Hummus Sandwich
- Grilled Turkey Burgers
- Chia Seed Pudding
- Baked Cod with Asparagus
- Roasted Brussels Sprouts with Balsamic Glaze
- Zucchini Noodles with Pesto
- Fruit Salad with Mint
- Low-Cal Chicken Pot Pie
- Grilled Portobello Mushroom Burgers
- Vegetable Minestrone Soup
- Spicy Roasted Sweet Potatoes
- Yogurt Parfait with Fresh Berries

Baked Zucchini Fries

Ingredients:

- 2 medium zucchinis
- 1/2 cup breadcrumbs (panko recommended)
- 1/4 cup grated Parmesan cheese
- 1/2 tsp garlic powder
- 1/2 tsp paprika
- Salt and pepper to taste
- 2 large eggs
- Olive oil spray

Instructions:

1. Preheat oven to 425°F (220°C). Line a baking sheet with parchment paper.
2. Slice the zucchinis into thin fry-like strips.
3. In a shallow bowl, mix breadcrumbs, Parmesan, garlic powder, paprika, salt, and pepper.
4. Beat the eggs in another bowl.
5. Dip each zucchini strip into the eggs, then coat with the breadcrumb mixture.
6. Place the strips on the prepared baking sheet and spray lightly with olive oil.
7. Bake for 20-25 minutes, flipping halfway, until golden brown and crispy.

Cauliflower Mac and Cheese

Ingredients:

- 1 head cauliflower, chopped
- 1 cup shredded cheddar cheese
- 1/2 cup grated Parmesan cheese
- 1/2 cup milk
- 2 tbsp butter
- 1/4 tsp garlic powder
- Salt and pepper to taste

Instructions:

1. Boil cauliflower until tender, about 8-10 minutes. Drain well.
2. In a saucepan, melt butter, add milk, and stir in cheeses until smooth.
3. Mix the cheese sauce with cauliflower, season with garlic powder, salt, and pepper.
4. Transfer to a baking dish and bake at 375°F (190°C) for 20 minutes until bubbly.

Turkey and Vegetable Chili

Ingredients:

- 1 lb ground turkey
- 1 onion, diced
- 2 garlic cloves, minced
- 1 bell pepper, chopped
- 1 zucchini, chopped
- 1 can diced tomatoes (14 oz)
- 1 can black beans, drained
- 2 tbsp chili powder
- 1 tsp cumin
- Salt and pepper to taste

Instructions:

1. In a pot, sauté onion and garlic until soft. Add turkey and cook until browned.
2. Add vegetables, tomatoes, beans, and spices. Simmer for 20-30 minutes.
3. Adjust seasoning and serve warm.

Greek Yogurt Pancakes

Ingredients:

- 1 cup Greek yogurt
- 1 cup flour
- 2 eggs
- 1 tsp baking powder
- 1/2 tsp vanilla extract
- 1/4 tsp salt

Instructions:

1. Mix all ingredients in a bowl until smooth.
2. Heat a non-stick pan and pour batter in small circles.
3. Cook each side until golden brown. Serve with toppings of choice.

Spaghetti Squash Alfredo

Ingredients:

- 1 spaghetti squash, halved and seeded
- 1/2 cup heavy cream
- 1/2 cup Parmesan cheese
- 2 tbsp butter
- 2 garlic cloves, minced
- Salt and pepper to taste

Instructions:

1. Roast squash at 400°F (200°C) for 40-45 minutes. Scrape out strands with a fork.
2. In a pan, sauté garlic in butter, then add cream and Parmesan.
3. Toss the squash in the sauce and serve warm.

Sweet Potato and Black Bean Tacos

Ingredients:

- 2 sweet potatoes, diced
- 1 can black beans, drained
- 1 tsp cumin
- 1/2 tsp smoked paprika
- Salt and pepper to taste
- Tortillas
- Optional toppings: avocado, salsa, cilantro
  Instructions:
1. Roast sweet potatoes at 400°F (200°C) for 20-25 minutes.
2. Mix roasted potatoes with black beans and spices.
3. Fill tortillas with the mixture and top as desired.

Chicken Zoodle Soup

Ingredients:

- 2 cups cooked chicken, shredded
- 4 cups chicken broth
- 2 zucchini, spiralized
- 1 carrot, sliced
- 1 celery stalk, sliced
- 1 garlic clove, minced
- Salt and pepper to taste

Instructions:

1. In a pot, sauté garlic, carrot, and celery. Add broth and bring to a boil.
2. Add chicken and zucchini noodles. Simmer for 5 minutes.
3. Season with salt and pepper.

Portobello Mushroom Pizza

Ingredients:

- 4 large portobello mushrooms
- 1/2 cup marinara sauce
- 1 cup shredded mozzarella cheese
- 1/4 tsp oregano
- Optional toppings: pepperoni, bell peppers

Instructions:

1. Preheat oven to 375°F (190°C). Remove stems and gills from mushrooms.
2. Spoon sauce into each mushroom cap, add cheese and toppings.
3. Bake for 15-20 minutes until cheese is melted.

Baked Apple Cinnamon Oatmeal

Ingredients:

- 2 cups rolled oats
- 2 apples, chopped
- 2 tsp cinnamon
- 1/4 cup maple syrup
- 2 cups milk
- 1/2 tsp baking powder

Instructions:

1. Preheat oven to 350°F (175°C). Mix oats, apples, cinnamon, baking powder, and syrup.
2. Pour in milk and stir well.
3. Bake for 30-35 minutes until set and golden brown.

Grilled Lemon Herb Chicken

Ingredients:

- 2 chicken breasts
- 1/4 cup olive oil
- 2 tbsp lemon juice
- 2 garlic cloves, minced
- 1 tsp dried oregano
- 1 tsp thyme
- Salt and pepper to taste

Instructions:

1. In a bowl, mix olive oil, lemon juice, garlic, oregano, thyme, salt, and pepper.
2. Marinate chicken in the mixture for at least 30 minutes.
3. Grill over medium heat for 5-6 minutes per side until cooked through.

Mashed Cauliflower

Ingredients:

- 1 head cauliflower, chopped
- 1/4 cup Parmesan cheese
- 2 tbsp butter
- 1/4 cup milk
- Salt and pepper to taste

Instructions:

1. Boil cauliflower until tender, about 8-10 minutes. Drain well.
2. Blend with butter, milk, Parmesan, salt, and pepper until smooth.

Tuna-Stuffed Bell Peppers

Ingredients:

- 4 bell peppers, halved and seeded
- 2 cans tuna, drained
- 1/4 cup Greek yogurt
- 1/4 cup diced celery
- 2 tbsp lemon juice
- Salt and pepper to taste

Instructions:

1. Mix tuna, yogurt, celery, lemon juice, salt, and pepper.
2. Stuff bell pepper halves with the tuna mixture.

Skinny Lasagna Rolls

Ingredients:

- 8 lasagna noodles, cooked
- 1 cup ricotta cheese
- 1/2 cup spinach, chopped
- 1/2 cup marinara sauce
- 1/4 cup shredded mozzarella
- Salt and pepper to taste

Instructions:

1. Mix ricotta, spinach, salt, and pepper.
2. Spread the mixture on each noodle, roll, and place in a baking dish.
3. Top with marinara and mozzarella. Bake at 375°F (190°C) for 20 minutes.

Avocado Toast with Poached Egg

Ingredients:

- 2 slices whole-grain bread
- 1 avocado, mashed
- 2 eggs
- Salt, pepper, and chili flakes to taste
  Instructions:
1. Toast bread and spread mashed avocado on top.
2. Poach eggs and place one on each toast. Season with salt, pepper, and chili flakes.

Creamy Tomato Basil Soup

Ingredients:

- 4 large tomatoes, chopped
- 1 cup vegetable broth
- 1/4 cup heavy cream
- 1/4 cup fresh basil, chopped
- 1 garlic clove, minced
- Salt and pepper to taste

Instructions:

1. Sauté garlic, then add tomatoes and broth. Simmer for 15 minutes.
2. Blend until smooth, stir in cream and basil, and season to taste.

Baked Falafel with Tahini Sauce

Ingredients:

- 1 can chickpeas, drained
- 1/4 cup chopped parsley
- 2 garlic cloves
- 1 tsp cumin
- 1/4 cup flour
- Salt and pepper to taste

Instructions:

1. Blend all ingredients until smooth. Form into small patties.
2. Bake at 400°F (200°C) for 20 minutes, flipping halfway.

Lightened-Up Shepherd's Pie

Ingredients:

- 1 lb ground turkey
- 1 onion, diced
- 2 garlic cloves, minced
- 1 cup mixed vegetables (peas, carrots, corn)
- 2 cups mashed cauliflower
- Salt and pepper to taste

Instructions:

1. Sauté onion, garlic, and turkey until browned. Add vegetables and season.
2. Transfer to a baking dish, spread mashed cauliflower on top.
3. Bake at 375°F (190°C) for 20 minutes until golden brown.

Quinoa and Veggie Stuffed Mushrooms

Ingredients:

- 8 large mushrooms, stems removed
- 1/2 cup cooked quinoa
- 1/4 cup bell pepper, diced
- 1/4 cup spinach, chopped
- 2 tbsp Parmesan cheese
- 1 garlic clove, minced
- Salt and pepper to taste

Instructions:

1. Sauté garlic, spinach, and bell pepper. Mix with quinoa and Parmesan.
2. Stuff mushroom caps with the mixture and bake at 375°F (190°C) for 20 minutes.

Banana Protein Pancakes

Ingredients:

- 1 banana, mashed
- 2 eggs
- 1/4 cup protein powder
- 1/4 tsp cinnamon
- 1/4 tsp vanilla extract

Instructions:

1. Mix all ingredients until smooth.
2. Cook in a non-stick pan over medium heat until golden on both sides.

Air-Fried Tofu Nuggets

Ingredients:

- 1 block tofu, pressed and cubed
- 1/4 cup cornstarch
- 1/2 tsp garlic powder
- 1/2 tsp smoked paprika
- Salt and pepper to taste
  Instructions:
1. Toss tofu cubes in cornstarch and spices.
2. Air fry at 375°F (190°C) for 15 minutes, shaking halfway through.

Chicken Lettuce Wraps

Ingredients:

- 1 lb ground chicken
- 1/4 cup soy sauce
- 1 tbsp hoisin sauce
- 2 garlic cloves, minced
- 1/4 cup water chestnuts, chopped
- Lettuce leaves

Instructions:

1. Cook chicken with garlic until browned. Add sauces and water chestnuts.
2. Spoon mixture into lettuce leaves and serve.

Whole-Wheat Veggie Pizza

Ingredients:

- 1 whole-wheat pizza crust
- 1/2 cup marinara sauce
- 1/2 cup mozzarella cheese
- 1/4 cup bell peppers, sliced
- 1/4 cup mushrooms, sliced
- 1/4 tsp oregano

Instructions:

1. Spread marinara on the pizza crust and top with veggies and cheese.
2. Bake at 400°F (200°C) for 12-15 minutes until cheese is melted.

Shrimp Stir-Fry with Brown Rice

Ingredients:

- 1 lb shrimp, peeled and deveined
- 2 cups cooked brown rice
- 1/2 cup broccoli florets
- 1/4 cup bell peppers, sliced
- 2 tbsp soy sauce
- 1 garlic clove, minced

Instructions:

1. Sauté garlic, shrimp, and vegetables for 5-7 minutes.
2. Add soy sauce and stir in brown rice.

Lentil and Kale Stew

Ingredients:

- 1 cup lentils
- 4 cups vegetable broth
- 1 onion, diced
- 2 garlic cloves, minced
- 2 cups kale, chopped
- 1 tsp cumin
- Salt and pepper to taste

Instructions:

1. Sauté onion and garlic, then add lentils and broth.
2. Simmer for 20-25 minutes, stir in kale and cumin, and cook 5 more minutes.

Grilled Salmon with Mango Salsa

Ingredients:

- 2 salmon fillets
- 1 tbsp olive oil
- Salt and pepper to taste
- 1 mango, diced
- 1/4 cup red onion, chopped
- 1 tbsp lime juice

Instructions:

1. Rub salmon with olive oil, salt, and pepper. Grill for 4-5 minutes per side.
2. Mix mango, red onion, and lime juice. Spoon salsa over grilled salmon.

Light Alfredo Pasta with Broccoli

Ingredients:

- 8 oz whole-wheat pasta
- 1 cup broccoli florets
- 1/2 cup Greek yogurt
- 1/4 cup grated Parmesan
- 1/4 tsp garlic powder
- Salt and pepper to taste

Instructions:

1. Cook pasta and broccoli until tender.
2. Mix yogurt, Parmesan, garlic powder, salt, and pepper. Toss with pasta and broccoli.

Sweet Potato Hash with Turkey Sausage

Ingredients:

- 2 sweet potatoes, diced
- 1/2 lb turkey sausage, crumbled
- 1/4 cup bell peppers, diced
- 1/4 tsp paprika
- Salt and pepper to taste

Instructions:

1. Sauté sausage until browned. Add sweet potatoes and cook until tender.
2. Stir in bell peppers and seasonings.

Eggplant Parmesan Stacks

Ingredients:

- 1 large eggplant, sliced
- 1/2 cup marinara sauce
- 1/4 cup mozzarella cheese
- 1/4 cup Parmesan cheese
- 1/4 tsp oregano

Instructions:

1. Bake eggplant slices at 400°F (200°C) for 15 minutes.
2. Layer eggplant, marinara, mozzarella, and Parmesan. Bake for 10 more minutes.

Veggie-Stuffed Bell Peppers

Ingredients:

- 4 bell peppers, halved and seeded
- 1 cup cooked quinoa
- 1/2 cup black beans
- 1/4 cup corn
- 1/4 cup salsa
- 1/4 tsp cumin

Instructions:

1. Mix quinoa, beans, corn, salsa, and cumin.
2. Stuff peppers with the mixture and bake at 375°F (190°C) for 20 minutes.

Black Bean and Corn Salad

Ingredients:

- 1 can black beans, rinsed
- 1 cup corn
- 1/4 cup red onion, chopped
- 1/4 cup cilantro, chopped
- 2 tbsp lime juice
- Salt and pepper to taste
  Instructions:
1. Mix beans, corn, onion, and cilantro.
2. Toss with lime juice, salt, and pepper.

Chicken and Veggie Kebabs

Ingredients:

- 1 lb chicken breast, cubed
- 1 bell pepper, cubed
- 1 zucchini, sliced
- 1/4 cup olive oil
- 2 tbsp lemon juice
- Salt and pepper to taste

Instructions:

1. Thread chicken and veggies onto skewers.
2. Brush with olive oil and lemon juice, season with salt and pepper, and grill for 10-12 minutes.

Butternut Squash Soup

Ingredients:

- 1 butternut squash, peeled and diced
- 4 cups vegetable broth
- 1 onion, chopped
- 2 garlic cloves, minced
- 1/2 tsp nutmeg
- Salt and pepper to taste

Instructions:

1. Sauté onion and garlic, then add squash and broth. Simmer for 20 minutes.
2. Blend until smooth and season with nutmeg, salt, and pepper.

Cucumber and Hummus Wrap

Ingredients:

- 2 whole-wheat wraps
- 1/4 cup hummus
- 1 cucumber, sliced
- 1/4 cup spinach
- 1/4 cup shredded carrots
- Salt and pepper to taste

Instructions:

1. Spread hummus on the wraps.
2. Layer cucumber, spinach, and carrots. Season and roll tightly.

Low-Cal Chocolate Mug Cake

Ingredients:

- 2 tbsp oat flour
- 1 tbsp cocoa powder
- 1 tbsp honey
- 1/4 tsp baking powder
- 3 tbsp almond milk
- 1/4 tsp vanilla extract

Instructions:

1. Mix all ingredients in a microwave-safe mug.
2. Microwave on high for 1 minute.

Greek Salad with Grilled Chicken

Ingredients:

- 1 grilled chicken breast, sliced
- 2 cups mixed greens
- 1/2 cup cucumber, sliced
- 1/4 cup cherry tomatoes, halved
- 1/4 cup feta cheese
- 2 tbsp olive oil
- 1 tbsp lemon juice

Instructions:

1. Toss greens, cucumber, tomatoes, and feta.
2. Top with chicken and drizzle with olive oil and lemon juice.

Sautéed Garlic Spinach

Ingredients:

- 4 cups spinach
- 2 garlic cloves, minced
- 1 tbsp olive oil
- Salt and pepper to taste

Instructions:

1. Heat olive oil and sauté garlic for 1 minute.
2. Add spinach, sauté until wilted, and season with salt and pepper.

Roasted Chickpeas Snack

Ingredients:

- 1 can chickpeas, rinsed and dried
- 1 tbsp olive oil
- 1/2 tsp smoked paprika
- 1/4 tsp garlic powder
- Salt to taste

Instructions:

1. Toss chickpeas with oil and spices.
2. Roast at 400°F (200°C) for 20-25 minutes until crispy.

Cauliflower Fried Rice

Ingredients:

- 2 cups riced cauliflower
- 1/2 cup peas and carrots
- 1 egg, beaten
- 2 tbsp soy sauce
- 1 garlic clove, minced

Instructions:

1. Sauté garlic, peas, and carrots. Add cauliflower rice and stir-fry for 5 minutes.
2. Push to the side, scramble the egg, and mix everything together with soy sauce.

Veggie and Hummus Sandwich

Ingredients:

- 2 slices whole-grain bread
- 1/4 cup hummus
- 1/4 cup cucumber slices
- 1/4 cup shredded carrots
- 1/4 cup spinach

Instructions:

1. Spread hummus on both bread slices.
2. Layer cucumber, carrots, and spinach. Close and slice in half.

Grilled Turkey Burgers

Ingredients:

- 1 lb ground turkey
- 1/4 cup breadcrumbs
- 1 egg
- 1/4 tsp garlic powder
- Salt and pepper to taste

Instructions:

1. Mix turkey, breadcrumbs, egg, and spices.
2. Form patties and grill for 4-5 minutes per side.

Chia Seed Pudding

Ingredients:

- 1/4 cup chia seeds
- 1 cup almond milk
- 1 tbsp honey
- 1/4 tsp vanilla extract

Instructions:

1. Mix all ingredients and let sit in the fridge for 4 hours or overnight.
2. Stir before serving.

Baked Cod with Asparagus

Ingredients:

- 2 cod fillets
- 1 bunch asparagus, trimmed
- 2 tbsp olive oil
- 1 lemon, sliced
- Salt and pepper to taste
- 1 tsp garlic powder

Instructions:

1. Preheat oven to 400°F (200°C).
2. Place cod and asparagus on a baking sheet. Drizzle with olive oil and season. Top with lemon slices.
3. Bake for 12-15 minutes until fish is flaky.

Roasted Brussels Sprouts with Balsamic Glaze

Ingredients:

- 1 lb Brussels sprouts, halved
- 2 tbsp olive oil
- Salt and pepper to taste
- 1/4 cup balsamic glaze

Instructions:

1. Preheat oven to 425°F (220°C).
2. Toss Brussels sprouts with olive oil, salt, and pepper. Roast for 20-25 minutes.
3. Drizzle with balsamic glaze before serving.

Zucchini Noodles with Pesto

Ingredients:

- 2 medium zucchinis, spiralized
- 1/4 cup pesto
- 1 tbsp olive oil
- Salt and pepper to taste
- Cherry tomatoes, halved (optional)

Instructions:
1. Heat olive oil in a skillet. Add zucchini noodles and sauté for 2-3 minutes.
2. Toss with pesto and season. Add cherry tomatoes if desired.

Fruit Salad with Mint

Ingredients:

- 2 cups mixed fresh fruit (e.g., berries, melon, pineapple)
- 1 tbsp honey
- 1 tbsp lime juice
- 2 tbsp fresh mint, chopped

Instructions:

1. In a bowl, combine fruit, honey, lime juice, and mint.
2. Toss gently and serve chilled.

Low-Cal Chicken Pot Pie

Ingredients:

- 1 cup cooked chicken, shredded
- 1 cup mixed vegetables (carrots, peas, corn)
- 1 cup low-sodium chicken broth
- 1/2 cup almond milk
- 1 tsp thyme
- 1 pre-made pie crust (or phyllo dough for lower calories)

Instructions:

1. Preheat oven to 375°F (190°C).
2. In a saucepan, combine chicken, vegetables, broth, almond milk, and thyme. Cook until heated through.
3. Pour mixture into a pie dish and top with crust. Bake for 25-30 minutes until golden.

Grilled Portobello Mushroom Burgers

Ingredients:

- 4 large portobello mushroom caps
- 2 tbsp balsamic vinegar
- 1 tbsp olive oil
- 1 tsp garlic powder
- Salt and pepper to taste
- 4 whole-grain burger buns
- Lettuce and tomato slices (for serving)

Instructions:

1. Preheat grill to medium heat.
2. Marinate mushroom caps in balsamic vinegar, olive oil, garlic powder, salt, and pepper for 15 minutes.
3. Grill mushrooms for 5-7 minutes per side until tender. Serve on buns with lettuce and tomato.

Vegetable Minestrone Soup

Ingredients:

- 1 tbsp olive oil
- 1 onion, chopped
- 2 garlic cloves, minced
- 2 carrots, diced
- 2 celery stalks, diced
- 1 zucchini, diced
- 1 can diced tomatoes
- 4 cups vegetable broth
- 1 cup pasta (e.g., small shells or elbows)
- 1 can kidney beans, rinsed
- 1 tsp Italian seasoning
- Salt and pepper to taste

Instructions:

1. Heat olive oil in a large pot. Sauté onion and garlic until softened.
2. Add carrots, celery, zucchini, and cook for 5 minutes.
3. Stir in diced tomatoes, vegetable broth, pasta, beans, Italian seasoning, salt, and pepper.
4. Simmer until pasta is tender, about 10-12 minutes.

Spicy Roasted Sweet Potatoes

Ingredients:

- 2 large sweet potatoes, diced
- 2 tbsp olive oil
- 1 tsp paprika
- 1/2 tsp cayenne pepper
- Salt to taste

Instructions:

1. Preheat oven to 425°F (220°C).
2. Toss sweet potatoes with olive oil, paprika, cayenne, and salt.
3. Spread on a baking sheet and roast for 25-30 minutes until tender and crispy.

Yogurt Parfait with Fresh Berries

Ingredients:

- 1 cup Greek yogurt
- 1 cup mixed fresh berries (strawberries, blueberries, raspberries)
- 1/4 cup granola
- 1 tbsp honey (optional)
  Instructions:
1. In a glass or bowl, layer yogurt, berries, and granola.
2. Drizzle with honey if desired. Serve immediately.

www.ingramcontent.com/pod-product-compliance
Lightning Source LLC
LaVergne TN
LVHW081341060526
838201LV00055B/2780